14 Real Life  powers

Activate Your Inner Superhero to Accomplish Your Goals and Live the Life of Your Dreams

M. D. MCGILL

ⓤ

Check out my blog, music
and social media sites.
Find me at
↓   ↓

www. Tridentlion. com

Table of Contents

A Dream About Empowerment

You are about to read a vital step in a young man's journey to find and discover a most wondrous treasure, the key to unlocking his real life super powers. All individuals have the capability to unlock their own internal super powers and to create positive self-empowerment. Examples of positive self-empowerment can be seen when someone achieves massive success, when someone builds the life they want. When utilized correctly, these real life super powers help individuals reach a state of empowerment, which is a force within each one of us that drives us to manifest our dreams and accomplish our goals. Empowerment radiates energy and sustains us through the day.

Now back to the young man's story... once he learns to embrace his own power, he is motivated to become a happier, smarter, and more successful individual. He realizes in order to do this he must first discover what his passions are and what motivates him. The young man wants to love all aspects of his life, to accomplish his goals, and to live out his dreams. One day, he discovers how empowerment works while dreaming. Upon waking, he writes down the dream and, in doing so, reveals the process of personal to himself. The dream is filled with vast amounts of information and knowledge, he discovers the secrets of how to build a life out of passion and love. He finds harmony with himself and his relation to his own sense of personal power. He is then able to utilize these various super powers to live out the life he has always dreamed of and to be the person he always wished to be.

On the night of the young man's memorable dream he was lying in bed, pondering his existence and visualizing his ideal life. He dreamt the life he desired, a life where he could make a living through his passion, which was playing music. As he was visualizing this, he drifted off to sleep. Coincidentally, his dream manifested as a vision of an orchestra playing music in a marble dome gazebo with striking bold pillars. The instruments were all arranged uniformly in a circle in the center of the structure. The gazebo was open and had five steps for each of the four entrances, it was tall and wide and radiated beautiful music. This music spoke to the young man's heart. The instruments were playing a remarkable harmonious symphony and he felt instantly connected. All at once, he felt the powerful emotions of inspiration, joy, and tranquility.

During the dream, the young man did not question what was happening because he was not conscious of the fact that he was dreaming. He perceived everything in his dream to be as real as anything else. For him, he felt the dream to be as ordinary as any other day with a heightened amount of joy and excitement. He didn't question the fact that the instruments were playing by themselves, or that once he stepped into the gazebo all the entrances turned into different projections of him living out different lifestyles. All he noticed was the sound of the music synchronizing with his emotions.

After hearing the music, the young man felt that the marble dome gazebo represented his connection to self-empowerment and akin to a source of infinite energy; one that could drive people to achieve massive life successes. The young man then began to ponder about what it would be like to have real life super powers. Almost instantaneously, he had the realization that this energy source and the idea of real life super powers were indeed related in some way.

As he thought about it more, he came to understand that the true nature of self-empowerment is formless, because it exists as an energy source inside of all people. Therefore, it is mutable and can morph into any form. Through sound and emotion, the young man was awakened to this idea, because music was his passion. Without any use of words, only through musical instruments he learned this; it was as if the instruments downloaded the information into his heart through music.

After several moments, the young man decided to play music with the instruments. A simple thought was all it took for him to conjure an instrument into his hands or on the ground next to him. He still didn't question his bizarre interaction with reality, he was asleep in a dream but everything felt real. He created instrument after instrument with his thoughts and every instrument he could think of appeared. He picked up a mandolin, and looked over at the hang drum, saxophone, and guitar that now sat next to him. It was thrilling to be able to play any instrument he could dream up, but he felt pulled to go play the beautiful crystal piano which sat in the center of the gazebo when he arrived. He sat down eager to join in with the harmonious orchestra, he closed his eyes to feel the music and struck his first note. He heard nothing. So he tried to play it again and he still heard nothing. He picked up and tried to play the banjo, the violin, and he even tried banging on the drums. It was as if everything in the hall had been paused or muted. He said to himself aloud, "why won't these instruments make a single sound? And why did the orchestra stop playing music? I very much was enjoying the music."

Then he heard a calm comforting voice say to him, "Because you must first understand what the instruments in this hall represent." He did not know where the voice was coming from, but before he could ask a question, even to himself, the cello from the hall hopped over to him and introduced itself. "You must first understand us, the instruments in the hall of self-empowerment. Greetings, I'm the power "courage" personified as a cello." He felt very surprised that a cello was speaking to him and he certainly was intrigued to have a conversation with a cello. Being that the cello said it was actually the power "courage" personified, he began to think of questions to ask. However, before he could articulate a question, a new sound gave him answers he didn't know he was searching for. "We are all in this gazebo of self-empowerment, which has been personified to fit your personal passion," said a floating saxophone, "what we really are is a collection of powers gathered together to empower your life." He started thinking about his personal journey, particularly with regards to how he'd been wanting to discover his passion in life, as well as discover real life super powers.

During the dream there was not much time for the young man to think. He was taking in so much valuable information and knowledge; he felt it was better to be like a sponge and soak up as much as he could.

"Do you want to know how to live the life you've always wanted, to be the person you've always desired to be?" Asked the saxophone. He responded with, "yes, yes of course, I have been seeking this knowledge for a while now." If the saxophone had a face, it most certainly would have had a smile on. "Before we explain anything to you. You must first promise to open your mind, heart, and ears, to what we are going to teach you. You must listen and give us your word that you will listen." He gave the saxophone his word. Then he turned his head 90 degrees to the right as the cello began to speak. "Also, promise to write down the knowledge we share with you, there is value in shared knowledge, and use in recorded information," said the cello. The young man gave the cello his word, and gathered the means to write it down. He manifested several fresh pages of parchment and a beautiful peacock feathered pen. The instruments asked him to create interviews and break them out into six sections.

Section 1.

    What is the superhero power of _____?

"This section will help you identify and understand more about what each power exactly is," said the saxophone.

Section 2.

    What benefits are there for empowering _____?

"Here we will elaborate upon why it is good to empower your real life superhero powers, and how it can benefit you," said the cello.

Section 3.

    Self-discovery with _____.

"This section is very important, it helps you find out your understanding and relation to each specific power being interviewed. Section 3 has open ended questions which you can ask yourself to discover how this power had aided you in the past as well as how you would like to utilize it to take your life closer to your dreams and goals. Be open to asking yourself even more question beyond what is in this section, questions which are relative to your personal situation. Use your imagination and ambitious desire to become more familiar with each power. This section will lead you in discovering more about you and how each power can aid, enhance, and improve you on your journey to success," explained the Piano.

Section 4.

> *Fun ideas regarding _____.*

"This section gives you something interesting, something fun, and maybe something new to think about in regards to each specific power. This can help your mind begin to think outside the box with regards to each power. Use your mind to come up with other fun ideas, metaphors, and/or analogies about the power. It will certainly help you understand at a much greater level." Said the Cello.

Section 5.

> *Daily practices to empower _____.*

"Section 5 will include several practices which you can do in order to empower each specific real life superhero power. Each power will contain various amounts of practices you can perform, however there are a massive amount of practices beyond what we will explain which you can do. It would be best to choose practices which are best for you. Use the examples to help yourself come up with additional practices which will work with your personality and lifestyle. Got it?!"

said the Guitar. "Yeah, I got it" said the young man with a smile.

Section 6.

Traits that signify an empowered _____.

"In section 6, we will provide various examples of a trait someone would have if they had one of their real life super powers empowered. When you read through the various examples you will find that you know people who have those traits. You'll even find various traits that you identify yourself to have and also traits you aspire to have." said the Drums.

Now that the young man had the interview structured he was ready, so he grabbed his peacock feather pen and parchment paper. The instruments explained how they were a representation of the force that moved the young man through his situations and circumstances in life. He was starting to realize that he had long forgotten the relationship with the potential of these powers. He realized that these instruments were actually the representation of those real life super powers he was seeking. As he interviewed each one of these powers, he felt as if he was being taught a wise life lesson by a cherished loved one. Each instrument identified which power it was representing; then explained its relation to him, and also to the other powers. He was learning how to empower himself and implement these ancient powers towards accomplishing his goals, and overall his success. He was very focused and determined to know all he could know about these real life super powers and the powers in his dream generously shared the information he was seeking.

At the end of the interview process he felt much more aware of these real life super powers and his relationship to them. He inscribed on the front of his writings a title and date. The inscription and date on the front of the writing was an indication that his work was finished for now.

Coincidentally, as soon as he wrote the title he awoke from the dream. He awoke feeling inspired yet calm. He slowly transitioned into an alert conscious state and remained in bed lying down, thinking about all the aspects of his dream. He felt he had learned a lot and he certainly hoped he'd remember everything. He decided to go write his dream down with a warm cup of coffee. As he stepped out of the bed he immediately realized that he was standing on a pile a loose parchment paper. The exact same parchment paper from his dream still containing all the information the powers, portrayed as floating instruments, had given him. He went through a series of dramatic emotions, envisioning his entire dream again until falling on his knees into the pile of parchment paper. The paper from his dream had traveled with him out of his dream. It was an act of magic.

He was baffled and convinced he was still dreaming. It took him awhile to reach the point of acceptance of the fact that the seemingly impossible had happened. At that point, he was relieved, and found it comical to be relieved, that he would not have to try and remember all the information and then write it down. He had given a cello his word after-all. At this, he remembered what the cello said about how there is value in shared knowledge. He was eager to share his new-found knowledge. He thought to himself, "I should read it first." So he picked up a random piece of parchment, it was the interview he had with the cello. However, it did not say cello, the parchment paper gave the cello's true identity, the cello was the power of courage. The first real life super power the boy read over that morning, was courage.

Courage

"All of our dreams come true if we have to courage to pursue them."

-Walt E. Disney

"Nature loves courage, you make the commitment and nature will respond to that commitment by removing impossible obstacles."

-Terrence McKenna

What is the superhero power of courage?

Courage is defined as the act of doing something that frightens you. When we are exerting our courage we are overcoming, breaking through, or disempowering a fear. John Wayne, the iconic American TV cowboy, once said "Courage is being scared to death, but saddling up anyways." Of course, there is a difference between courageous and stupid, which can be recognized in the reason behind the action. The idea is to utilize this energy to propel you towards your dreams and to aid you in the process of accomplishing your goals. One of the greatest foes we have, which works against the accomplishments of our goals and dreams, is fear. Far too often people have allowed fear to consume them. Use courage like a machete. Use it to cut through the forest of thick thorn bushes you have created from fear. Use it to get to the other side of the forest, to get to the clearing bereft of self-imposed obstacles. Use it to get to the clearing that is your paradise. What is paradise? In this analogy paradise is you living the life you want to live, being the person you desire to become, and being as successful as you hoped you be.

What are the benefits of empowered courage?

Having courage in relation to accomplishing goal is like needing gas for a car to get you to a destination. Courage is a candle light in a dark room clouded by fears. Courage gives you the ability to navigate through a world of worry, like windshield wipers in a thick storm. Courage clears your view from the millions of rain droplets of worry, allowing you to push forward towards your destination. The absence of courage would put anyone at the mercy of their own fears. The absence of courage would also bring a journey of desires and goal accomplishing to a screeching halt. Similar to a car in a rain storm without any windshield wipers; you would bring your car to a screeching halt.

Courage allows you to overcome challenging obstacles. Without courage most difficult obstacles, those you desire to overcome, won't even be attempted. Empower your courage and make an agreement with yourself that you will not let challenging obstacles discourage you, or take you off track from accomplishing your goals. If your fail, choose to perceive it differently. Perceive it as a new beginning, where you can choose to give up or to reset and try again. A lot of people succeed after several new beginnings. I feel the reason is because their understanding and experience with what they want to succeed in, is training them for success.

Courage builds your confidence, allowing you to be more expressive. A lot of people have insecurities, such as public speaking, and some fear human interaction or being alone. By empowering your courage, you will give you the strength and confidence to communicate and express your ideas, points, and beliefs to others. Courage can liberate us from our fear. For example, if a person is terrified to public speak, but needs to do so for professional reasons and they follow through with it, then it is an example of empowered courage. If they speak publicly a few more times and become accustomed to it, the less afraid they are of it. And with consistent strength to not give in to the fear, the fear becomes weaker and weaker. So weak and long forgotten that the person who once feared public speaking goes on to become a master at public speaking. Hence, courage can liberate you from your fears.

Self-discovery with courage:

You can ask yourself the questions below to learn about your own sense of courage. They should serve to awaken the courage within you and allow you to individually assess your situation in a more impactful manner.

In what ways am I courageous?

In what ways am I NOT courageous?

What fears am I holding onto that stop me from being courageous?

How do these fears serve me?

How can I strengthen my courage now?

How can my courage serve me when handling my passions and goals?

Is there a specific area of my life I can use more of the power of courage?

Is there anyone I admire for their courage? Why do I admire them?

Fun ideas regarding courage:

Some people find it to be a struggle when removing personal fears. A very common example of this is the fear of failure. Imagine avoiding something simply because of a fear of failing. The immediate quitting attitude is an automatic fail. If someone wants something bad enough in their life, they cannot be scared of failure. Embrace fear of failure as a part of the path to success. The fear of failure is a challenging test of will.

This test of will can be explained through a story of a man named Warren. Warren was in search to become the world's greatest alchemist. For Warren, success would be accomplishing the talent, skill, and recognition to achieve the title of "The World's Greatest Alchemist." However, Warren had a fear of failure and he could choose between two paths; path number one, Warren could pursue his passion for alchemy and overcome his fear; path number two, he could never pursue his dream of becoming "The World's Greatest Alchemist," letting his dream always remain a dream. Failure was possible through either one of Warren's paths, however, only one path had the possibility of success. For Warren, to choose path number two would be an act of betting against himself, and it was a guaranteed loss. So Warren chose path number one, to

venture off on his journey to become "The World's Greatest Alchemist." For Warren, he felt the second path would only bring him regret and the annoying question to forever ponder; the question of "what if I chose path number one."

Now you have these same paths to choose from with regard to your dreams. You don't have to think that choosing to chase your dream means sacrificing everything else in your life. Someone might say that they can't act upon their highest excitement and passion because they don't have the time. Or they make excuses that they can't follow their passion now because they need to do something for money now. These are normal and valid concerns but you can still do what you need to do to survive while pursuing your dreams. By making a small time commitment each day to the realization of your goals, will amount to incredible progress.

Courage is like a muscle, but one of the mind and it needs to be exercised to work properly and occurs within people via thoughts and feelings. The idea is to radiate as much courage as possible, to increase courage of the collective consciousness. Courage and can have a snowball effect. Roll the snowball of courage across a yard, allow it grow and expand and become capable of breaking through any fear.

Daily practices to empower courage:

A great way to strengthen your courage is to go after what it is you're afraid of, without causing harm to

others and/or yourself of course. If you have stage fright, then find some way to put yourself in an acting class. If you have a fear of heights, then go skydiving or visit the Grand Canyon. Strengthening courage, as previously mentioned, requires you to confront and challenge your deepest fears. The biggest challenge in conquering your fear is identifying the fear, and, more importantly, identifying the root cause of the fear. If you're afraid of public speaking, try to figure out the reason why you're afraid of projecting yourself to a crowd. Is it because you are scared of people, failure, or embarrassment? Maybe it's all of these things together, maybe something that only you can know. Once you know what the true root cause of the fear is, you can completely remove it from your mind. It is like removing weeds from your garden, if you rip it apart from the stem, it will grow back fast. But if you remove the weeds from their roots, you kill the weed.

Courage can be compared to a sword. Use it to guard against, conquer, and release one of your worst enemies, fear. If the fear emerges again, recognize that it is there and then let it go. You can be the sunshine of your life, providing sunlight to only the plants in your mind which you want to see grow. The sunlight you radiate is your attention. Avoid the weeds of fear and allow your strengths to thrive, in the beautiful garden of your psyche.

Traits that signify empowered courage:

You are fearless when pursuing your dreams.

You have faith in yourself.

You take action upon your dreams.

You are good at setting goals and accomplishing them.

You are confident.

You are a leader.

Knowledge

"An investment in knowledge pays the best interest."

-Benjamin Franklin

What is the superhero power of knowledge?

Knowledge can be defined as an awareness discovered upon by experience and/or fact. Most people just get it, knowledge is an understanding. One can memorize concepts and/or facts, however, a new-teenaged-driver can memorize facts for a written test on how to drive. The teenager will only be knowledgeable on how to drive after they fully experience it.

What are the benefits of empowered knowledge?

Knowledge can connect you to your life, those around you and your environment. When you commit to deep, comprehensive learning, you will function and maneuver more adeptly through the course of your life.

For example:

A person's knowledge of how to change a tire is beneficial when someone has a flat tire.

A polyglot uses his knowledge of language to the benefit of communicating with others, and the polyglot learns norms, behaviors, and belief systems from other cultures. With that knowledge the polyglot can better understand, sympathize, and relate to a wide variety of people.

A chef with the knowledge of food benefits others by preparing delicious meals for a variety of diets.

A plumber, having the knowledge of septic systems, will benefit everyone with running water and toilets.

A chemical engineer, with the knowledge of how to create medicines, can benefit many who are sick.

Self-discovery with Knowledge:

Knowledge is so vast it can be challenging to distinguish, what is valuable knowledge? What is relative knowledge? How should we define wisdom and information in comparison to knowledge? What is accurate knowledge? And so on. Questioning can improve your understanding and use of the power knowledge. It is a birthright to decide to pursue knowledge in what you are passionate about.

I hope the questions below help you discover more about yourself. They may reveal truths or confirm what you already know; they may also give insight into more of what you want to know. The more you learn about yourself, the more accurate the knowledge you pursue in life will be relative to your strongest passion. Use the power of knowledge to create more questions which dig deep into your mind and you will unearth your life's truest mission.

How has knowledge served me?

What knowledge do I desire?

What topic do I get excited to learn about?

What knowledge do I need to attain to aid in the manifestation of my goals?

What do I wish to be more knowledgeable about?

What do I enjoy talking about with others?

Fun ideas regarding knowledge:

The absence of knowledge is a dark silly state known as ignorance. Ignorance is dark because, when one is ignorant, they are blinded, unable to see or understand what's in front of them. Knowledge is like a candle flame in a dark room, aiding one in becoming aware of their surroundings. Ralph Waldo Emerson, the famous writer/philosopher of the 19th century, said that, "knowledge is the antidote to fear". Several times it is in our ignorance that we become fearful.

In order for knowledge to stick, it is either learned through experience or it is a topic of interest that ignites our passion.

We all must learn the difference between information and knowledge, as Albert Einstein once said, "Information is not knowledge", and being able to regurgitate back facts and figures does not make one knowledgeable.

A fun concept of knowledge is that it is non-local information stored in the database of the universe. Knowledge is surrounding us at all times and it is our job as receptors to pick up on it, similar to a car radio picking up on various AM/FM stations. We must "tune-in" to the right station in order to acquire the knowledge we are searching for.

Daily practices to empower knowledge:

Set goals for yourself. Physically write out what you want to accomplish, and be as specific as possible. Have a time limit as to when you would like your goal to be accomplished. Have long term goals and many shorter term goals that will take you where you want to go, step by step.

Read a book or listen to an audiobook (preferably on a subject relative to what your interesting in learning). Learn, explore, entertain, and be inspired by others through the books they have written. Audiobooks are a great way to fit reading into a busy schedule. Listen to an audiobook when you are driving and/or going to sleep. Read books as much as you can. Books are a great insight into the experiences and understanding of others. You can learn a lifetime of experience and knowledge in a single book. Read even if it's for only 5 minutes a day. A consistent effort will keep you moving on the road toward attaining the knowledge that you are seeking. Learn with an open mind and feel encouraged to ask and have questions.

Pick up and practice a foreign language. Learning a new language is a great way to expand your knowledge. If you do, try to learn at least one word a day, and be persistent every day. Learning another language will broaden the range of people you can interact with as well as aid in building a strong resume if you happen to be in the process of starting a new career.

Pick up and master several artistic practices like writing, music, painting, and sculpting. Make progress towards the knowledge you want to attain and be persistent.

Listen to others public speak. Watch lectures, listen to podcasts, and attend seminars. Absorb as much valuable information as you can.

Look for others that are experts in the field of knowledge you're seeking; if you can, go talk to them. You can ask the expert to be your mentor, ask the expert questions, learn from them, and realize they are living a success story in your particular field of study. If you're lucky, you may even find someone close-by who is doing exactly what you want to be doing. See this, and know you can allow this success to be possible for you as well.

You can also go to school online or in-person. Going to school can help structure topics you wish to learn. You can also meet and surround yourself with others who are learning the same topics as you. Some people dread the idea of school because they associate school with being bored, likely because their past experiences in this setting is filled with learning (or avoiding) a subject of no interest. Imagine going to a class to learn about a subject or topic which greatly interest you. How would your attitude be different? By doing this school can seem and be more enjoyable.

Think about any of the challenges or struggles in life where you acquired the help and assistance of others. Then think about what challenge or struggle you wish you were able to do yourself. For example, you may never have a desire to learn about a septic system and hiring a plumber may be easier for you. However, maybe you wish you knew how to change a tire rather than calling a friend or relative to go out of their way to assist you. There are certain areas of knowledge which we are proud to outsource to others and they are able to make a living off of this. Then there are other areas where lack of knowledge may be burdening those around us and making us feel powerless. A great benefit to empowering your knowledge is that you are expanding upon what you can do, which would; increase your confidence, and make you an ever more valuable connection to others in the game of life.

Traits that signify empowered knowledge:

People look to you for knowledge and information.

You understand the ins and outs of your craft.

You have others come to you for advice.

You are open minded.

You help others reach a state of clarity.

Imagination

"Imagination is not only the uniquely human capacity to envision that which is not, and therefore the fount of all invention and innovation. In it is arguably the most transformative and revelatory capacity, it is the power that enables us to empathize with humans whose experiences we have never shared."

-JK Rowling

"Logic will get you from A to B, imagination will get you everywhere."

-Albert Einstein

What is the superhero power of imagination?

Imagination is the animation of our thoughts and feelings. Many dictionaries choose to define imagination as the ability to see things that are not real within the mind. This is an interesting way to describe it, being that many things in our imagination have happened and/or will happen. For example, you can imagine a previous encounter with a close friend from a year ago, or you can imagine your dream career, and that dream career may actually blossom into a reality. These are just two examples of how your imagination may serve as a catalog, containing a vast array of feelings and imagery, sometimes providing people with a vision of their past and/or a window to a spectrum of possible futures.

The imagination has a lot to do with working with the law of attraction. For those that are unaware of the law of attraction, it is a commonly accepted belief that we attract experiences into our lives based on what we have thought. Think of the imagination as a database of infinite possible futures that gives us a preview of each possibility we choose to explore. The possibility that comes into manifestation, out of the large array of choices, is conjured because the individual that envisioned it backed it up with the greatest amount of conviction and/or held the largest amount of faith in that possibility to be the outcome. People do this all the time whether conscious or unconscious.

What benefits exist for empowering imagination?

By empowering your imagination your mind will become more open, better able to perceive others' situation by allowing you to see yourself in their shoes. Though this will not get you to fully understand someone 100%, it is a common practice among amiable and compassionate people who attribute this practice to making the world a more unified, loving place. Having an empowered imagination helps when, consciously or unconsciously, you are conjuring up a new idea. Think of all of the wonderful ideas that people have brought into manifestation. Different ideas and inventions within medicine, technology, politics, education, and so on were first just a thought within the mind. All of the most brilliant, average, and silly ideas came from the imagination of an individual.

Our imagination also gives us the ability to self-reflect. We have the ability to reflect upon who we are, what we want to do, and what makes up both our passions and our fears. We can all humbly imagine ourselves as an improved, better version of us. Each one of us can become better at something in our lives as long as we can imagine it and we should express gratitude towards our imagination for this gift. With an image and an idea in mind of the person you wish to grow into, you will always better your chances of becoming that person.

Many people wish to improve themselves. They want to find better job, to lead a healthier lifestyle, and to live in a way that fulfills all their needs and desires. In a nutshell; the ideal life is to love your work, love your body, and love your life. Fortunately, we can all imagine a more positive and empowered life for ourselves. This is the first step; the next step is to take action towards becoming *your* desired version of you. For too long and too often, people imagine situations, jobs, health, experiences, and other things that they do NOT want. We, as people, sometimes feel weakened by our fears, and our worries to the point where we mistakenly take on these fears and worries, then proceed to mold them into our belief system. This is a very common yet dangerous practice. We always have a choice when it comes to perspective, as well as what we consciously want to imagine. Our fears and worries sometimes trick us into forgetting that we have power.

Compare a vision of a worry and a vision of a desire. In your mind, would you rather vison something you do not enjoy or vision something that you do enjoy very much. It's that simply of a choice. We all have the power to choose what videos we put in front of our eyes, which media we tune into, and which program we consume. The same is true with what we consciously project into our minds every day and when we take time to think about our lives. It is also true when we imagine and when we dream.

This is a good practice: throughout the day, notice your thoughts and build upon or change them to suit your needs and desires. Notice yourself on autopilot and be proud of yourself for having unconscious positive thoughts and visions. If your autopilot mind is negative, recognize it, contemplate upon why you feel that way, and simply ask yourself if the negative thought or vision you have is worth sacrificing your well-being, and if it helps you in any way towards self-empowerment or achieving your goals.

Self-discovery with imagination:

Answering the questions below may help you to expand your thinking and free yourself of burdensome unconscious limitations. The hope is that you become more aware of yourself, so you can better align with your dreams, goals, and desires. A Q&A, is a fun exercise, where you can dig for golden nuggets of truth and reveal buried aspects of yourself. These will serve as important tools for the creation of your personal experience.

What do I see when I imagine my desires?

What does my ideal/dream life look like?

What does my ideal/dream life feel like?

Is there something that I cannot imagine?

How does my improved version of me look?

How does it feel to interact with others in my ideal world?

Can I imagine living in a more positive and harmonious world?

Fun ideas regarding the imagination:

The imagination is like the internet and our individual minds are like our laptops and desktops. We can tap into the infinite realm of the imagination at any time and once in a while we bring something into reality from the imagination. People have conjured many great inventions, ideas, social norms and so on from the imagination.

Daily practices to strengthen imagination:

The imagination can, and usually is, used in every possible place and at every possible moment. The only time people possibly will not use it is when they are good at a mindful practice like meditation, which can silence the mind and, in a way, power off the imagination. One of the best times to exercise the imagination is in the shower. We all, for the most part, shower daily so imagination strength training is easy to incorporate into most people's lives. When you shower your mind and body are both relaxed, calm and loose. You are free from the daily stimulations, obligations, actions, decisions, and so on. When you shower you get a break from external stimuli and you can turn your attention to your mind. Envision a goal, or strong desire of yours, then envision it manifesting into reality. This is one of many fun and easy practices that you can incorporate into your life.

Another fun thing to try practicing is the art of visualization. Visualize something creative, funny, happy, inspiring, or whatever floats your boat.

You can also do something creative, and artistic. You can write a short story, or even paint a picture of an underwater sea fairy castle, it's up to you. Expressing your creative side can be very soothing, fun, and rewarding.

Traits that signify you are empowered through imagination:

You are prone to optimistic beliefs.

You are an exquisite problem solver.

You have a strong connection to your creativity.

You experience a variety of conversations and activities.

Patience

"Patience is bitter but its fruit is sweet."

~Aristotle

What is the superhero power of patience?

Patience is the capability of remaining in a positive or neutral state while tolerating delays, misfortunates, accidents, and any other period of time between what you desire and manifesting your desire. Patience can also be perceived as a capability to endure trouble, delay, or suffering without getting upset.

Leonardo da Vinci, one of the most famous figures in history, had to attain a lot of patience throughout his life. He needed patience with regard to both his artwork and his inventions. In his writings, Leonardo da Vinci had this to say about patience,

"Patience serves us against insults precisely as clothes do against the cold. For if you multiply your garments as the cold increases that cold cannot hurt you; in the same way increase your patience under great offences, and they cannot hurt your feelings."

Try to wear patience like a full suit of armor and protect yourself from any negative criticism when pursuing your goals, passions, and dreams. Use patience when dealing with what you perceive as faults and criticisms from others. Also be sure to have patience with yourself. Sometimes we can be extremely negative towards ourselves. Patience helps keep you focused and on track with your goals, passions, and dreams. This is why it is an important power to wield because at any moment those dark forces of criticism, doubt, and discouragement may attempt to persuade you into giving up on your dreams. Wield the power patience to endure any of those dark forces which may attempt to knock you off of your path to success.

Patience can be used and is generally needed every day. Patience is a powerful muscle that gives you the power to better maintain and control your emotions. Too often we allow ourselves to let external forces change our emotions, forces such as circumstances, people, and environments. Sometimes we allow the things that we can't control, control us. Patience can help liberate us from our unconscious habit of sacrificing the emotional state we prefer for one that we do not prefer.

What are the benefits of empowered patience?

Having patience will help you remain calm and on track when handling hard work or when dealing with failure.

If you have children, wielding the power patience can make you a better parent. A parent who can wield the power patience and tame negative emotional outburst tendencies is both more respectable and more secure in the eyes of their children. It will also teach children how to wield the power patience for themselves. Kids seem to never do what their parents tell them to do, but they seem to do what their parents do.

Wielding the power patience can help you improve your relationship to your work and the environment in which you work.

Patience aids in interactions, allowing us to coexist in a positive and constructive manner.

By wielding patience you can help liberate yourself from several mental illness. One such mental illness that specifically heals from being empowered with patience is anxiety. Anxiety saps the energy of our mind and body, so learning to be patient can really help balance your entire being.

Self-discovery with patience:

Answering the questions below may help you to understand your relationship to patience. These questions can be wonderful tools to help you navigate through your mind and self-discover. Ask yourself the questions, and respond to your questions sincerely and then come up with a few of your own questions. Try to make questions relevant to your life and/or your current situation involving the power of patience.

In what situations do I lose my patience?

What do I gain by losing my patience?

How can patience better serve me?

Is there any person or situation I wish I generally had more patience with?

Has there been a situation in life where I wish I had been more patient?

Fun ideas regarding patience:

Patience has this coin of control about it, sort of a yin-yang to it. On the one side, it requires a sense of control over emotions. On the other side, it seems to require the opposite of control; it requires the accepting that part of it is out of your control. It requires letting go and allowing what you are patiently waiting for to manifest. Hold on to your emotions, let go of trying to make things happen.

It is interesting to try to manage different aspects of patience in life. It can be hard to tell when it's okay to lose patience and push forward and when it's best to call on more patience. This relies heavily upon how you feel about the situation. For example, if you're in an abusive relationship, it would be best to avoid being patient with them and get out of the relationship, however, it is good to think about patience with regard to the belief that everything will be okay. Once you take that brave first step, new opportunities will undoubtedly fall into place.

Utilizing patience is paramount when pursuing a dream. Imagine someone's dream is to become a legendary musician. The process and pursuit of their dream will require a lot of patience if they actually want to manifest themselves as this. It would be counter-productive to lose touch with patience and give up. In fact, Benjamin Franklin once said "He that has patience can have what he will." He said this to emphasize the importance of patience whilst in the pursuit of your dreams. We can accomplish our goals, pursue our passions, and live out our dreams as long as we have the patience to attain them.

Patience also works very well with other superhero powers for example, patience and persistence are very compatible powers and are used together frequently. One should be patient when being persistent, and also be persistently patient when pursuing their goals, passions, and dreams.

Daily practices to empower patience:

The idea is to be patient everyday, anytime you feel yourself to be anxious or in a hurry, just breathe, and take it as a challenge. A challenge to overcome the emotional self-mutilating behavior we can sometimes put ourselves through. Some traumatic things in life are very hard to be patient with, and requires a great deal of emotional strength to overcome, but more commonly we deal with miniscule problems that require patience. It is with these situations that we slowly build our power patience and where it is necessary that we maintain a positive attitude and have a proper composure. For example, not getting upset over traffic, or not getting upset you haven't won a lottery jackpot, not getting upset because your food is taking too long, or not getting upset because the oil change in your car is taking too long. All of these examples are situation and interactions in our day to day life where are patience is challenged. Each one of these interactions you have throughout the day allows you the opportunity to strengthen your patience. By choosing to empower patience, you allow yourselves to reduce your suffering in those moments when patience is challenged. The more patient you are the less suffering you will experience. So on a daily basis be consciously aware of yourself and situations where you feel yourself to have an absence of patience. Then, when you're in that situation, make a conscious effort to wield more of the superhero power patience. By doing this everyday, you will start to notice yourself becoming more at peace.

One of the most recognized practices to empower patience is meditation. Meditation helps quiet your whole being and strengthens your patience in both your subconscious and conscious mind. Having busy lives, we manifest busy minds and meditating can be a powerful exercise for taming this. When the mind is silent we preserve our energy.

Spend time around children. Go babysit a friend or relative's child. Being with kids can be an extreme test of patience. I'm sure your parents can tell you all about it if you don't have any kids of your own!

Take on a goal that challenges you. If you encounter failures on your road to success, stand your ground, be persistent, patient, and know that success is inevitable as long as you do not quit. Failures, no matters how big or small, seem to be inevitable when pursing a goal. However, success, also seems to be inevitable as long as you have the patience to never give up.

Traits that signify empowered patience:

You are calm and tend to calm others.

You maintain a positive state throughout the ups and downs of your day.

You live in the present, and are grounded in the moment.

You are content.

You understand that some things in life require time.

You are compassionate and understanding to others.

Gratitude

"The struggle ends when gratitude begins."

-Neale Donald Walsh

"Don't cry because it's over, smile because it happened."

-Dr. Seuss

What is the superhero power gratitude?

Gratitude is defined by a feeling of thanks and/or a feeling of appreciation. The superhero power of gratitude is one's capability to constantly reinforce what it is they are grateful for. Gratitude can be perceived as an art form, in which one must perform a ritual around the affirmations of gratitude.

What are the benefits of empowered gratitude?

A few meaningful benefits to an empowered sense of gratitude are joy, contentment, emotional well-being, and a simultaneous growth of patience.

Gratitude helps people figure out what they want in life, what they want more of in life, and what they want to change about their life. Without gratitude people may never know what they want, leaving them feeling discontent. This is because, without gratitude, if someone receives something that they wanted they won't appreciate it, thus leaving them with the same feeling as before, discontent. So award yourself by feeling grateful, unhappiness is too heavy of a burden to carry and it can remove one from the here and now. Let's look at this with an analogy of a movie film. The beginning may be slow, you might not enjoy some of it but you heard it was a great movie and told a friend you'll watch it. Would you rather fast forward through the movie, skipping scenes and quickly going through it? Or do you feel it is better sit back, relax and enjoy the movie?

Similar to life, you can sacrifice your contentment or state of being present, to fantasy and envy all of which you don't have. Or instead, you can ground yourself in the here and now, appreciate everything that's special to you, and trust yourself with accomplishing your goals, desires and dreams.

By empowering your gratitude, you can become more grounded and present in your life. You may find that with daily gratitude, you have less tendencies to contemplate the past and/or future. Gratitude can be used like an anchor for a boat with the boat as your mind. The superhero power of gratitude can anchor you in the now.

Self-discovery with gratitude:

Gratitude is important for all of us to have, gratitude helps us to live with contentment. Sometimes we may lose track of our expression of gratitude. I ask myself these questions to better understand my relationship with gratitude. You can create some of your own questions that are relevant for you. Do some self-discovery; explore what you're grateful for, and feel the feeling of appreciation.

What am I grateful for today?

In what way am I grateful for circumstances that have been difficult for me?

How are things better today?

What everyday things do I take for granted?

Is there anything I appreciate, but tend to lack appreciating?

How can I become more grateful in my life?

How do I feel when I feel grateful?

Fun ideas regarding gratitude:

Working with the power of our thoughts and emotions; living with the law of attraction, we must find the things that we once wanted, and appreciate having them now. Focusing on what we have already brought into our reality will instill trust that your dreams can manifest. Gratitude makes what we have, worth having. If you crave a food that you don't have access to every day, the time building up to eating the craved food is filled with so much excitement, and joy. Then once you eat it you feel so happy and grateful to be eating it. For example, gratitude will help preserve all of those positive feeling while you're eating the sushi as well as when you've finished the sushi. Those that disregard gratitude are toying with themselves and constantly teasing themselves; they are merely chasing after something only to be disappointed again once they have it.

Daily practices to empower gratitude:

Use gratitude as often as you can. You can practice gratitude whenever you have alone time with yourself. Go through and say all the things that you are grateful for no matter how minute or grand they may appear to be. When you say, out loud or to yourself, all that you're grateful for, radiate the feeling behind why you're grateful for it. The more frequent you feel grateful now, the more frequent you'll feel grateful in the future. You can analyze and feel all of the things you happen to be grateful for in the shower, in the car, in bed, while you're in the bathroom, you can be anywhere and express gratitude—it is a very easy habit to pick up.

Give gratitude to others by sending a text or a letter to someone. Explain to them why you are grateful to have them in your life. Another act of gratitude you can do for a friend or relative whom you feel gratitude for is to buy them a gift, a nice dinner, or a service such as a massage or yoga class. Sometimes when you yourself provide the act of service for them it's the perfect way to say thank you. One great idea a child can do for their parents is to complete all their chores and more without having to be told to do so. A boss of a company can express his gratitude towards his employees by submitting raises, giving out bonuses, rewarding outstanding work with recognition, and/or throwing a company party.

Practice emitting the feeling of joyful appreciation of what you have and of what you want. Imagine the feeling of having what you desire right now.

If you want something try to tap into the vibration of having it already. Visualize and analyze anything you will soon be grateful for, this is a fun and healthy practice.

Throughout your day, look at actions done by yourself, others, and nature which you truly appreciate. It can be as minuscule as someone holding the door or as grand and cliché as being thankful for your mom for giving birth to you.

A great way to empower your sense of gratitude to find what you appreciate about yourself. The more you recognize and express the aspects of yourself which you are grateful for, the more others will recognize and express their gratitude for you. Put gratitude into practice as frequently as possible.

Traits that signify empowered gratitude:

You give thanks to all that you appreciate.

You are content and joyful.

You are in harmony with your life.

You continuously receive more abundance.

You say thank you on a daily basis.

Giving

*"We make a living by what we get,
but we make a life by what we give."*

-Winston Churchill

What is the superhero power of giving?

Giving can be defined as the transfer of something for free. It may be a transfer of an object, and also a transfer of someone's time for labor or advice.

What benefits are there for empowering the act of giving?

The act of giving is the warm satisfying feeling you when you offer something to a person and feel that it's the right thing to do. It can create unconditional love during a moment of time between people. There is great power in giving, Anne Frank, who lived during a time of massive suffering, had this to say about the power of giving, "no-one has ever become poor by giving." Giving needs to be accomplished from a balanced place, however. When you want to give, try not to give beyond your means. It can be counter-productive to give to the point of harming yourself.

To give to another in need sends a big message to the universe. The message says that you live in a constant place of abundance. You are filled with so much abundance inside of you that you are overflowing, and choosing to fill others with abundance as well. The person who is timid and scared to give is usually a person who is tortured by their fear of possible scarcity. By empowering your ability to give you can aid in the process of harmonizing your relationship to abundance. You do not have to be the biggest philanthropist in the world to be a hero either. Very small acts of giving can banish the dark shadows of pain, fear, hunger and poverty; like a tiny wooden matchstick illuminating an entire dark room. It was Mother Teresa who said, "If you can't feed a hundred people, then just feed one." By increasing you power to give, you simultaneously grow in value. Like Mother Teresa advising to feed just one person, if you feed someone who is painfully starving, your gesture of giving will be the most valuable gesture that painfully starving person received. Even giving just a few seconds of your time, to hold a door open for a handicap person, or to help a mother struggling with three toddlers and arms full of groceries, or to give a smile to someone who looks like they need a pick-me-up. All of these acts you can do, would be uplifting and valuable to others. In return your mind and spirit will be uplifted as well to a more positive state.

Empowering your ability to give engages you positively in the concept of paying it forward. Through our experiences we can come to the conclusion that every action has a reaction, what you emit into the universe, you get back. So the act of giving is like a boomerang and it can bring back to you what you are giving. I think an important aspect to this process is how you feel. If you feel you would be hurting yourself by giving, then it would be counter-productive to give. Maybe you don't have the money, the right knowledge, or the proper means to give at that moment in time in a particular way. The power to give works positively and most effectively when you are able to give without having yourself fall into a state of suffering. When you're feeling content and feeling right giving, then give.

In order to engage and strengthen the power to give, you must feed it the proper fuel. You must feed it a positive vibration and feeling. Without those two ingredients the power of giving may backlash against you, it may conjure more suffering.

Of course, the strongest and most impactful way to give is to give unconditionally. Coincidentally, those that give unconditionally are, in fact, existing in that state of abundance and emitting out positive feelings towards giving. Some people who exercise the power to give unconditionally, perceive giving as an aspect of their life, making it feel as normal and correct of a habit as eating food or drinking water.

Giving can also help you overcome hoarding tendencies, both the hoarding of material things and the hoarding of emotional things. The ability to let go can be attributed to the power to give. If you don't practice letting go, holding on will seem all the more normal and can become a vicious habit. In Buddhism, a basic principle is, attachment leads to suffering. So whether you're a Buddhist or not the principle makes sense and we can all relate to the uncomfortable feeling we get when we lose something we are emotionally attached too. With an empowered ability to give, you grow in your capability to let go. Letting go is a useful skill to have living in a material world because there is so many materials to get attached too.

Those that can't let go may tend to burden themselves with a cluttered house full of garbage, useless things they do not need. They tend to burden their minds by holding on to feelings from the past. The power to give can help you not just through aiding the needs of others but by releasing things from your possession and control which you do not need. It can be quite astonishing witnessing the speed of which someone will de-clutter, reassess, and fix their computer when it starts acting up and how slowly, if at all, someone will proceed with de-cluttering, reassessing and fixing their mind.

Utilize the power to give by de-cluttering any messes in your environment and mind. Give away all that you no longer have any use for; give your burdening thoughts and emotions away to the universe. When you hold on to unwanted feelings about the past, such as regret, depression, anger, blame, you can become weighted down and ill. The remedy would be to engage the power to give and release these feelings from the past and for the future out to the universe. Holding onto negative feelings from the past is like watching a sad movie where you learn the lesson in the movie, you feel the sad feelings from the movie, and decide to hold onto those feeling long after the movie has ended. Ask yourself, are these burdening emotions from the past more valuable than my preferred positive state, right here in the present moment?

The power to give can also strengthen the bonds and bridges we have to our peers and community. We construct bridges and relationships when we lift others up through giving; we aid in the general abundance of the human collective. The world can be a calmer, more positive place if we learn to lend a hand to others, and to clear out our own burdens which we may have stored deep within our minds.

Self-discovery through Giving:

Here are a few questions that helped me better understand myself with regard to the superhero power of giving. I hope that, by asking yourself these questions, you discover your true feelings about your ability to give. You may rediscover a fact about yourself which you appreciate and you may discover truths about yourself which you would like to change.

When I give away something, am I doing it expecting something in return?

How do I feel after I give someone something unconditionally?

What can I do to start feeling good about giving today?

How can I give to others in a way that will help them?

In what way do I feel I give a lot?

In what way can I give more?

How comfortable am I with giving?

Fun ideas regarding the power giving:

The act of giving is seemingly an unconscious consistent theme in our day to day life. We give time to one another, we give out food to friends and family, we give compassion when another person needs it. However, we do have our challenges when it comes to conscious giving. Many people are hesitant with regards to giving when it comes to money. We may think some don't deserve to be given money. We also may think the thought of, what will this person do for me in exchange for what I have given them? Handing someone something and expecting something in return is not an act of giving, it is a barter, trade, or sale.

Daily practices to empower giving:

You should try and find various ways in which you can incorporate giving in your life. For example, if you work with other people you can unconditionally buy others coffee or lunch. The next time you find yourself in a work environment, make a choice to give something of value to another. Your act of giving doesn't have to be limited to coffee or food, try giving another help with a project, advice with something you excel at, or simply give someone the time to listen to them.

Give your attention and ears to another and listen to what they have to say. Sometimes the only thing someone wants is attention and to be heard. If you give someone your attention and listen to them sincerely, you will certainly help brighten their day. By doing this, you will become more comfortable with the power to give. People will also respect and like you much more if you are fully present. We all know how annoying it is to be around people who only talk about themselves and never listen.

If you have children you can give them the greatest gift possible...time. Incorporate your schedule and day towards spending it with your children. By giving your children more time with you, you will most likely discover that you simultaneously gave yourself something valuable and rewarding. This can be said for time with other loved as well. Spending time with your parents, siblings, friends, and even pets can be a great gift of giving, because some people don't know how much you love and care for them until you actually show it. Let them see that they are important to you, take time out of your busy schedule to prioritize your loved ones.

If you are having challenges or blockages with giving you can do some self-discovery and analyze any beliefs, blockages, or feeling you may have regarding the act of giving. Not all situations and circumstances call for you to give something, sometimes it may be best to give nothing. Knowing when to give and not to give can be a challenge in itself. Before I make my decision to give, I consider a few basic thoughts and questions like: Is this act of giving ethical or moral? Is the situation an urgent one? Would this be giving within my means? Does it feel like the right thing to do? Most likely, if all those questions are considered a yes, then I will give unconditionally, expecting nothing in return.

We strengthen our emotional connection by giving away any burdening feelings we have whatever you believe in or whatever gives you strength beyond yourself. This can be a god or goddess, source, mother nature, or the universe. So the next practice is to give away, release from your mind, all of the unwanted feelings, beliefs, and thoughts. Liberate your mind, and allow yourself to exist in a more tranquil, positive, and free state of mind. A great way to release these unwanted things is to stop giving them attention. Once you do this, those unwanted feelings, beliefs, and thoughts will fade from your experience.

Traits that signify empowered giving:

You are nurturing, kind, and compassionate towards yourself and others.

You make others feel comfortable.

You sacrifice time and resources for others in need.

You are someone who likes to share.

You tend to be praised with gratitude.

Receiving

"If you wish for light, be ready to receive light."

-Rumi

What is the superhero power of receiving?

Receiving can be defined as an act of getting, or being given something. We all attain things, things like objects, money, time, or advice. Two important factors contribute to the power of receiving, one is your ability to feel you deserve it and two your ability feel grateful for it.

Our connection with the power to receive, may not always be aligned with our wants. Some people, without the understanding of the power of receiving, are given things by default. People receive things and respond in a manner that is a result of their programming, conditioning, and habit. For example, some people turn down offers throughout the day because they have been conditioned to respond quickly, to quickly blurt out "no thank you." However, what these people may be thinking is, "thank you for being kind, however, I can't take this because I have nothing to give you."

Some people can be conditioned to the point of losing touch with a relative aspect of reality. The aspect of reality I'm referring to is when people give and receive to others unconditionally. Some people have a tendency to lose touch with this factory, but it should be viewed as a blessing in both directions. It is a blessing that you are abundant enough to give out of the goodness of your heart unconditionally. When you are receiving something unconditionally it is also a blessing.

What benefits exist for the empowerment of receiving?

Receiving is a great power to improve upon because it is a constant act in our life. It is good to not just feel grateful and joyful when receiving things, but to also be aware of what it is you're receiving. On many occasions we receive something for which we have no need. Instead of perceiving it as a burden, you can find someone who does need it and give it to them. The benefit of receiving something you don't need is that you become overabundant in an area in your life; this allows you to pass it on to another who actually does need it. For example, if you are given a brand new computer for your birthday and you're not so sure how to feel about it, because you already have two, you can give it to a loved one who doesn't have one. Many people in the world are, unfortunately, less abundant and each day, we can put in some effort, however great or small, to help alleviate some of their suffering. I feel it is a mistake when we receive something we don't need and get upset about the matter, I am guilty of it myself. Anyone who has experienced an overabundance in an area in their life may think or act like a spoiled child. Nobody thinks it is cute when a bratty spoiled kid is freaking out because the car his parents bought him was dark red rather than bright red.

Receiving is an important power, especially with regard to abundance. Sometimes people build barriers and blockages in their lives, which, prevents abundance from coming to them. Imagine if you lived by a river and every gallon of water that flowed by your house paid you ten dollars. Everyone would love that, right? The river would be providing you with passive free income, and you would receive it in abundance daily. So with a situation like that, would you wake up one morning and say "enough with this river, I'm going to go build a large dam and stop this river from flowing past my house"? It would be super silly for some to even say that but several people do that with their mind. The universe delivers ideas, opportunities, and circumstances to us and we build up mental dams in our minds. We prohibit ourselves from receiving abundance which is all around us. These blockages or dams can take on several forms and will vary from person to person. Examples of these can be old beliefs system, a built up habit, maybe even a closed mind. So a tremendous benefit to having the empowered ability to receive can be massive abundance flowing freely into your life.

Self-discovery about receiving:

These questions can help you discover your relationship to the power of receiving. Hopefully by doing some self-discovery you will reveal to yourself any blockages you might have. Once you have recognized these, you can choose to liberate yourself from them, thus creating a smoother flow of abundance pouring into your life. You can also personalize questions that are specifically relevant for you. I believe we deserve to achieve our goals, attain our desires, and live out our dreams. We need to be ready, and in a state of allowing in order for those things to be received. Any resistance whether, conscious or unconscious resistance, may deflect those things from you.

When I am given something do I accept it gratefully?

Do I feel uncomfortable when I receive something?

Am I allowing things to be given to me unconditionally?

Do I feel I need to give something in return when I receive something?

Do I believe that I deserve to live the life of my dreams?

Am I open to an infinite array of abundance channels?

What do I normally say and do when given something?

What type of blockages, if any, prevent me from receiving?

Fun ideas regarding receive:

It seems we are receiving things all the time in our lives so why not empower our ability to receive things in a more proper, conscious, and positive manner? The superhero power to receive is a crucial power in the process of manifesting your dreams. Your ability to wield this power will be a deciding factor whether you do or do not manifest your dreams. You can work hard for a long time and manifest nothing if you struggle with this ability.

Daily practices to empower the act of receiving:

This first practice takes us back to the benefits section of receiving, when I talked about the blockages and dams people build up in their minds. Take time to analyze and discover what these look like for you. Once you have recognized it, find a way to let them go. Allow the rivers of abundance to flow into your life. Understand that it can be challenging to get rid of blockages. For some individuals these are a belief system they've had ingrained for their whole life. Constructing a completely new belief system is difficult, but well worth the effort. A great method to aid in the process of breaking down a strong barrier is to evaluate it and place a value on it. Ask yourself, how has this old belief system served me? Is it more valuable to keep, or dispose of it?

The power of receiving may happen at any moment and at any time. Another valuable method to practice the power of receiving is the use of visualization sessions. Purposely daydream, visualize a desire or goal you have and then feel yourself receiving it. Use the power of imagination to help you practice and empower your ability to receive. Imagine yourself receiving advice from one of your role models, practice expressing the power of gratitude, feel joyful, and believe you deserve it. Imagine yourself having it right now, and believe it!

Start to become conscious of the moments when you are given something, observe your behavior and thoughts. Start taking the time to process how you feel and what you think. You may feel grateful, joyful and even feel you deserve it. In this situation, during your time of self-reflecting, congratulate yourself and strive to keep that attitude consistent. You may also feel a certain level of discomfort when you are given something. Once again, observe your thoughts, emotions, and actions during this act of giving another has bestowed upon you. If you feel any discomfort, take some time to discover its root cause. Then ask yourself, is the root cause of my discomfort worth feeling uncomfortable about? Does the overall feeling of discomfort enhance my life, or provide any value in my life?

Start practicing the art of asking, because with asking comes receiving. You can ask friends, co-workers, family, and the universe for anything. You won't necessarily get everything you ask for, but if you want something, you have to ask. Think about when you go out to get food, you always ask for what you want to eat, and then you receive it. If you want ketchup or mayo for your fries, you have to ask for it. There are an innumerable amount of things you may ask for. You may ask for advice, help, a new car, a new job, or money, but to receive it, you must first ask. Sometimes in order for us to receive something we desire, all we have to do is simply ask for it. If you ask for something and you do not receive it immediately, then use it as a goal to work towards. As long as you keep your eyes on the prize, never give up, and maintain a goal which you believe is possible for you to achieve, then whatever you asked for, you most certainly will receive.

Traits that signify you are empowered with the ability to receive:

You attain your desires easily.

You are an appreciative gift getter.

You feel you deserve to have health, happiness, and abundance.

You find it easy to ask for things.

You allow things to come to you.

Emotion

"Love is the only force capable of transforming an enemy into a friend."

- Martin Luther King Jr.

What is the superhero power of emotion?

Emotions are comprised of the vast spectrum of human feelings. Emotions are what make up the majority of the way we communicate and interact with one another. Emotions are a valuable power because if utilized effectively, they can propel you towards your goals and dreams. However, when this power is not utilized properly, it may propel you in the opposite direction of accomplishing your goals, and fulfilling the life of your dreams.

What benefits are there for empowering emotion?

Learning to understand your emotions is a great way to discover what you love and don't love, what you want and don't want, and what is and is not important to you. With this type of knowledge attained within you, you can better assess your situation and maximize on what would be the best life for you.

The superhero power of emotion can also help you connect and communicate with others via feelings. Think about when you communicate with someone, you communicate more with emotion than with words, whether you realize it or not. The power of emotion is not consciously utilized as much as it could be with regard to connecting and conversing with others. Conversing and connecting to others unconsciously is very common, oftentimes throughout our day, we are actually on emotional autopilot. I have experienced as well, but it wasn't really until I started working in sales that I truly learned how to connect with people emotionally. Enhancing your own and others' emotional wellbeing is such an amazing practice and habit. Be conscious of the emotions you and others radiate, and when conversing, attempt to bring about a harmonious state. Sometimes, certain situations or circumstances may require you to provide a more quiet space, so you save the conversation for a better day. Little or no words are sometimes the best medicine.

Questions about emotion you can ask yourself:

Here are a few questions I tend to ask myself about my emotions. I use these questions, amongst others as a way to become more familiar and in tune with the superhero power of emotion. I hope you find these questions helpful and then ask yourself additional questions which are personal and relative to you.

How often am I conscious of the emotion I am radiating?

How often am I conscious of others' emotions?

What scenario do I wish I had a better grip on my emotions?

How can an empowered understanding of emotions serve me?

How can my empowered understanding of emotions serve others?

Do I often get angry/sad/upset/overwhelmed for reasons I do not always understand?

If I am misplacing my emotions, what area of my life am I suppressing them?

What emotions do I prefer? Which emotions do I not prefer?

What are my favorite emotions? How can I feel more of them?

Fun ideas regarding emotion:

Our emotions can be perceived and used as tools, a compass to navigate through life and towards our goals, desires, and dreams. I believe both positive and negative emotions can be used as learning experiences. We all feel difficult emotions from time to time. When we are in a bad mood we can decide to clean up and clear out the buried darkness within us. In this mode of negativity, try to utilize the power of action and courage to liberate yourself from some suffering you may be experiencing. For example, if you are prone to jealousy, discover why you feel jealous, ask yourself if feeling jealous is benefiting you in any way.

Discover the inner fears and unconscious beliefs and then make a conscious choice to clean up your mind and clear out those negative tendencies. To let go of a negative emotion, find out the root cause and then confront it. Watch yourself for a couple of weeks and log what you notice a journal. Over the years you may have picked a variety of emotional patterns, but if you identify the source of these emotions, you can prevent them from creeping up in your mind. You will move one step closer to eliminating that habit from your life. Ask yourself if that negative habit is creating some sort of value in your life, most likely it's not, so you need to find ways to diminish its power over you.. Imagine hiking with a heavy backpack up a mountain, and you recognize the root cause of your heavy back pack is a 40-pound rock that someone put in your backpack without you realizing. A giant rock just taking up a lot your energy, back pack space, and slowing down your hike. How long would it take for you to remove the 40-pound rock? Maybe only a couple seconds after you say to yourself, "Wow, this is why my back pack feels so freaking heavy." That 40-pound rock might be a large negative vibration burdening your mind.

Our beliefs, environments, experiences, and thoughts all have the potential to put negative seeds into our mind. A negative seed can grow a big negative tree that stretches out roots into the depths of our minds, but only if we allow them to. We can decide at any moment to confront the beastly tree and remove it like a gardener removing unwanted weeds from his/her vegetable garden. Once you have identified a negative belief or thought, you can make a choice either to let it grow or eliminate it.

Emotions can be viewed as fuel for the power of action. If someone is experiencing challenges with their power of action, they can use their power of emotion to sometimes do the job of the power of action. People seem to take action based on either emotions or logic. Emotions allow the power of action to make choices based upon a strong desire or a strong fear. Logic is usually taking action based on the best "odds in your favor," calculated choice. Emotions are a powerful tool that each of us has and because they are tools they are neutral. Emotions alone are not exclusively positive or negative, but they are a combination of the two. As we have all experienced, our tools of emotions can cause bliss, horror, and everything else in-between.

Daily practices to empower your emotion:

Throughout the day, keep a mental inventory of your emotions and thoughts and monitor them. When a positive emotion enters your day, welcome it, cherish it, and embrace gratitude towards it. When a negative emotion enters your day, do the same thing. Do not fight your negative emotions or run away from them. Instead welcome your negative thought and emotion in like a guidance consoler welcoming in a difficult child. Go ahead and discover the root concern, fear, problem, or whatever negative emotion is haunting your moment by asking questions to yourself regarding the emotion and its relation to your life. Find out if the negative emotion contains any sufficient amount of value, making it worth keeping, and expressing, in your life.

Another easily and extremely enjoyable practice to strengthen your power of emotion is to dive into music. Play music, sing, dance, or even listening to music will certainly aid in the strengthening of your emotions. Music has the power to bring our emotions out into our experience, the more we experience our emotions the more we can understand them. Music can also be used as a remedy to balance out our emotional state. Music can help walk us through our negativity, as well as lift us up to a preferred positive state.

When you interact with others try to uplift their emotional state. Find emotional harmony with others, which helps enhance everyone involved. Compare this to a song. In a song there are several instruments and what makes a songs great is how the instruments can play together. Think of a song that makes you feel incredible. Now imagine if you could replicate that incredible feeling when you interact with others. On the contrary think about how some human interactions are simply unenjoyable. This is like a bunch of kids playing random instruments for the first time, out of rhythm, out of tune, and out of harmony. Think of a child that is randomly slamming his hands and fingers on the piano keys. Know the child wants to be able play a beautiful symphony, he just hasn't learned how to yet. People have this conversation every day, they would like to have social interactions go well but they haven't learned how to yet. Sometimes we are like the kid that slams his hands on the piano.

Practice sitting and meditating, find your center. Go through your relationships and circumstances and verbalize any thoughts you do not prefer about them. If an issue arises to your attention during your meditation, recognize the difficult feelings and release them.

Traits that signify your emotions are empowered:

You can easily discover the cause and reason for your suffering.

You are a compassionate person.

You are direct and honest with your feelings.

You are strong and willing to express yourself.

You can easily release unwanted feelings.

You can relate to others easily.

You are conscious and present with your emotions.

Creation

"*Creativity is the power to connect the seemingly unconnected.*"

-William Plomer

What is the superhero power for creation?

Creation, is the superhero power defined as an act of bringing something into existence. When you create you conjure something which wasn't previously there. The power to create can be brought to existence by the combination of two other powers, the powers of action and imagination. The superhero power to create can be perceived as your personal alchemy kit. Alchemy has been described throughout history as the act of transforming lead into gold. The power of creation is most easily recognized by our physical activation of it, like transforming a blank canvas with paint materials into a beautiful piece of artwork. It is also often used non-physically, like how we have the power to transform a negative mood into a positive mood. With our creativity we can shift are mind from one state to another.

What benefits are there for empowering creation?

Empowering your ability to create can help you become an efficient problem solver. Sometimes we need to think outside the box when solving various problems in our lives.

Empowering your creativity may increase your ability to socialize, like coming up with analogies and metaphors to help others understand you. Our power to create works in harmony with the power of speech craft. These two separate powers align, in synchronicity, for the joined purpose of creating conversation.

The power to create can allow you to express yourself to others using several different means. For example, if you want to express gratitude towards a loved one or co-worker, you can create a thank you card, you can create a party for them, or create a cake for them. Wielding the power of creation can open up a vast array of options for you to pick from when deciding how you wish to express yourself to another person.

Self-discovery with creation:

Below are a few questions you can ask yourself to discover the truth behind your current relationship with the power of creation. These questions, amongst several other questions, can help you organize, evaluate, and recalibrate your relationship with the power to create. The idea is to discover a way for you to become more harmonious with this power and utilize it to propel yourself towards your goals, desires, and dreams. Use your power to create to come up with your own questions as well, ask yourself questions that are relative to your life's story.

How has creativity served me in life?

What do I enjoy doing which requires me to be creative?

What do you appreciate in your life that has been created by another?

Has there been any situation where I wish I had been more creative?

How can I be more creative?

Who do I admire whose success is attributed to the power create?

Fun ideas regarding create:

The ability to create is like an act of magic. Bringing something from nothing into existence. I find it interesting and fun to compare the creative process to energy and matter. Science describes matter as being non-physical, matter is simply condensed energy. Similar to something which has been created like an electric car, children, a popular song, a rocket, a pencil, these are all expressions of our superhero power to create. Art, technology, ideology, these are all examples of condensed imagination, which were combined with action to be expressed and experienced by others.

Our imagination supply an infinite source of information. We each have the power create within us, this captures and pulls ideas out of our imagination into physical reality. This is like the Wright Brothers discovering the concept of airplanes in their imagination, then using their power create to manifest the first airplane. The 20th century author, William Plomer, beautifully described the power create in a simple manner. He said, "Creativity is the power to connect the seemingly unconnected." This quote correlates well through to the perception that the superhero power to create stems from the superhero power imagination. The superhero power to create connects ideas in the imagination to the physical plane, which sometimes may seem unconnected. Again, much like the Wright Brothers' vision of an airplane, it seemed impossible to some people. Skeptics could not connect the brothers' imagined idea of a plane with reality. With the power to create, the Wright Brothers connected the seemingly unconnected; the invention of the airplane, and our reality. It's amazing what the power create can do, very few people could have envisioned our ability to fly across the world in a large heavy tub and believe it to be possible. Most people thought it was impossible because of the law of gravity, and the superhero power to create, once again, granted us the impossible.

Daily practices to empower creation:

Find time to do something creative during the day, something you enjoy. This practice will be rewarding, not only because you will be building a stronger creative muscle, but rewarding because it can be fun. For example, my sister's favorite creative medium is drawing. She loves to draw, particularly with markers, and she has been doing it since she was a young child. She finds drawing to be a great way to reduce stress. The power to create can be utilized in several aspects of our life. My sister's strengthened creativity from drawing has spread to an improved creative outlook in other areas of her life, other areas such as writing essays for school and being creative with conversation. By strengthening our ability to wield creativity through an enjoyable daily habit, we will discover our power to create has improved in areas beyond our daily habit.

Make up stories about strangers in your head. You can do this while driving, while at the store, or at a restaurant. Look at someone whom you've never meet before and come up with a fun story about them. You don't have to talk to them however the act of coming up with stories does exercise our power to create so have fun with it! This practice will also aid in strengthening the power of imagination too.

Observe and ponder what people do every day, then find out what you feel is ridiculous and funny. Come up with a joke about the thing you find funny, even if you're not a funny person, create a joke that makes you laugh. This practice can be a mood enhancer while empowering your ability to wield the power create.

A general practice, which many people do on a daily basis while in pursuit of their dreams, is to build and contribute to their dream. Look at the example of a young man who dreams of opening his own coffee shop. This young man is dedicated and determined to manifesting and maintaining his dream. On a daily basis, this young man contributes and builds to his dream, one step at a time. He finds the perfect location, he creates the perfect atmosphere, and he hires the perfect team of employees to help build and share his passion with world. This process of building and continuously working towards your dream ultimately leads to the creation and manifestation of your dreams. So, the superhero power to create really can help you accomplish your goals.

Traits that signify an empowered ability to create:

You are a great problem solver.

You are a master of your craft.

You can easily express to others what you experience in the imagination.

You have crafted works of art which you and/or others appreciate.

You can turn a bad situation into a great one.

Awareness

"To become different from what we are, we must have some awareness of what we are."

-Bruce Lee

What is the superhero power of awareness?

Awareness can be defined as the state of condition or being which you have knowledge, you're conscious, and cognizant. Those who are empowered in their awareness have a deeper understanding of something. For example, a firefighter has a strong power of awareness with regard to fire. If a building is on fire, the firefighter's knowledge, experience, and materials may be enough to put the fire out. The firefighter's empowered awareness is utilized when needed to contain a dangerous, life-threatening fire. Throughout this section you'll encounter two types of awareness. The first type is the awareness of yourself and the present moment. The second type is the awareness of something which is external from you, like the firefighter using his awareness to put out a fire, the fire is external from the fire fighter.

What are the benefits of empowered awareness?

Becoming more aware can release burdens which you may have bestowed upon yourself, burdens in the form of dangerous daily habits which you may not be fully aware of. For example, eating/drinking unhealthy foods (essentially starving your body of nutrients), speaking negativity about yourself or others, and watching an excess of television are all common dangerous habits that often go unnoticed. These examples, among countless others, are essentially destructive behaviors which weigh many people down.

If you want to manifest and live out your dreams, it is necessary for you to start eliminating habits which may be holding you back.

Many people lose touch with the present moment. They split their awareness into two directions: One is to gaze upon the past and remember and reminisce. The second is to gaze towards the future; dreaming, fearing, anticipating, predicting, and expecting. Most of us do a mix of both, but by empowering your awareness, you may experience a lesser amount of your time that otherwise would be swept up by the past and/or possible futures. If you are someone in pursuit of your dreams, living in the now is beneficial because it helps slow time down. Being in the now eliminates time spent thinking about the past and future. You can put that extra time to use, work towards actualizing your dreams and move closer to your goals.

Empowering your awareness can aid in the empowerment process of other powers as well. The superhero power of awareness helps us empower all of the other powers. Awareness does this because it helps us understand each of our powers by being aware of ourselves and our relationship to each power. The more awareness you have—the easier it will be for you to wield its power.

Self-discovery with awareness:

The power awareness can be a challenging power to work with. People sometimes direct their power of awareness towards something which is not a joy to them, they are living just to survive. By becoming aware of what you really want in life is one of the greatest treasures you can discover for yourself. I hope these following questions based on awareness will help you discover yourself, so you can uncover where your attention flows.

What I am exceptionally aware of?

Am I aware of what my passion is?

What area in my life do I wish to be improve with awareness?

How can I empower awareness?

What do I desire to become aware of?

Fun ideas regarding awareness:

Within all of us is an aspect referred to as our observer side. There is a part of us that is observing every action we take, and emotion we feel. The observer side of us is fully aware of what is happening and observes unbiasedly—it is free of emotion. When you observe yourself in this way, you are stepping outside your self, so you can witness your life from an outsider's perspective.

Think about when you encounter a unique situation. Try using awareness is two different ways. First, be aware of a situation and how you feel about it. Second, be aware of a situation without any emotions involved. How did you experience multiple perspectives about the exact same situation? What did your mind perceive? This exercise can help open your mind to the reality that with every single situation there is an infinite array of perspectives.

Daily practices to empower awareness:

Meditation is a wonderful practice which anyone can do. Sit still, quiet your mind, and allow your awareness to expand. A simple meditation to practice requires focus to the breath. During inhalation expand your stomach, as if filling yourself up. During exhalation contract your stomach. This focus on the breath will help quiet the thoughts and help strengthen your awareness, bringing you a little more presently in the now.

Visualize and meditate. Another fun and impactful meditation is to imagine abundance, health, and joy with every inhalation. Imagine what those things mean to you filling you up, imagine them becoming a part of you. Then when you exhale imagine all the suffering you might be feeling in your life, imagine yourself exhaling it out of you. The more suffering you release the more room you have for joy, abundance, and health. Release any burdens from your life, become present, and breathe.

For those of us who may not have the time, quiet space, or a strong ability to wield the power of patience in order to sit still and meditate; you can instead do a daily practice known as noting. This practice can be done all day long and requires no separation from your daily activities. As you go throughout your day, be aware of yourself doing things. Be the observer to your life. Be present with your body while you wash the dishes, do the laundry, play with your kids, whatever activity you find yourself doing. Turning our focus to the present moment can help pull ourselves back into our body, and out of the chaos of our thoughts. This practice gives us more connection to ourselves and those around us, thus making us fully present. This meditation is most helpful when experiencing heightened emotions. Being present and observing the emotion, acknowledging that you feel the emotion without acting on it, is a path in the quick course to becoming more aware.

Dancing and singing are both fun and impactful activities which can ground you in the present. You can even play music if you have the means and desire to play an instrument. If you do not like playing instruments or singing, then definitely try dancing. Put on a piece of music you enjoy and dance in any manner, have fun and be free to dance no matter what you or others think.

You can also play sports. Sports are fun tools that help us calibrate our awareness. Playing a sport can help ground you in the now. When you play a sport, you usually do not think about anything else besides the sport you're playing. Notice which activities that usually quiet down and ease your mind; these are activities will undoubtedly benefit your awareness.

Take up a hobby. For example, take a yoga class, sign up for a book group, art class or 5k fun run; start taking music lessons; enroll in a pottery class or group sport. Concentrate on the present while you do this new hobby or activity, it will most likely enable you to feel more grounded and peaceful.

Ask yourself or others questions about a topic you are interested in and would like to use an awareness building tool. This is simply an example to describe the process of becoming more aware of something through questions.

Traits that signify the empowered ability to be aware:

You are in the moment.

You may have a very good memory.

You are not easily distracted.

You may also have a strong power of patience.

You are very knowledgeable in some fashion.

You can understand the point of view from another's perspective.

Communication

"In making a speech one must study three points: first, the meaning of producing persuasion; second, the language; third the proper arrangement of the various parts of the speech."

-Aristotle

What is the superhero power of communication?

People that are excellent communicators can be exceptionally persuasive, likable, witty, and creative. When considering a profession where communication is being utilized, most think of media, sales and law. It is true that reporters, salespeople and lawyers exercise their superhero power of communication regularly, because their job often depends on it. However, anyone can benefit from the power of communication.

Imagine working a job at a coffee shop or a bar. You work with people and talk all day and night. You can choose to not empower your communication and treat every customer the same. You could express yourself as a mundane, repetitive drone. We all have experienced these people, whether at a food establishment, a hotel, or through a customer service experience. We have conversed with another whom is not personal or non-emotional. On the contrary, we have experienced people who are personal, friendly, and funny.

So imagine working at that coffee shop, you have a choice. You can be unemotional, mundane, and boring or you can choose to empower your communication and wield it to make the day or night better for everyone, including your boss and co-workers. When you open up to others and converse, you never know where an encounter with another may take you.

What are the benefits of empowered communication?

If you have an empowered communication ability you can communicate and connect with people easily. You can open doors for yourself and others just by talking and sharing with the best intentions at heart. You might be able to converse your way into landing a dream career, convincing a crush to go on a date with you, or inspiring others, to follow through with tasks efficiently. We interact with others on a daily basis. By utilizing your ability to charm, you will find more examples specific to your life where you will get what you want.

The superhero power of communication can be used to give you a stronger presence and to help you express yourself while conversing with another. Be conscious that communication can also be used negatively to manipulate, control, and persuade others against their will. Always strive use this superhero power for good.

One of the biggest fears in the human collective is public speaking. However, the more empowered one's communication skills become, the more fear is shed. When you have empowered communication you can be both impactful and efficient while following through with a public speaking tasks. You become more efficient because you can address your material in a clear manner and you become more impactful. Talking from your heart is a key component to any great public speech. When you really make an impact on someone, it is generally because you have addressed their feelings through your words. Think about any great speech you've ever heard, or think about a time when you listened to a motivational speaker. Think about those experiences when you've observed a master of public speaking and communication, almost every one, if not all, of those experiences, impacted you on an emotional level.

Self-discovery with communication:

Communication is a wonderful superhero power to strengthen, especially if you deal with people daily. These question may help you to better understand your position with the superhero power of communication. Do some self-discovery and come up with questions that are specific to you. Think about all the situations in your life when you found communication to be helpful and when you found yourself in need of empowered communication. Find out how you can utilize the power of communication so in can be of better service to you. Harness this great ability to bring yourself closer to accomplishing your goals, desires, and dreams.

How can empowered communication help me in my life?

How has communication served me?

Who or what comes to mind when I think of a great communicator?

When has communication not in my favor?

Am I communicating with others as best as I would like too?

Fun ideas regarding communication:

Communication is similar to the idea of magic spells. People often view magic spells as being negative, and they certainly can be negative and used for selfish reasons. However, they can be used for good as well. Imagine a person, maybe a comedian, someone who goes through life placing magic spells on others for the sole purpose of make another feel happy. The ability to make someone happy with only the use of words is a beautiful gift.

Daily practices to empower communication:

If you work with people, you are already exercising your communication muscles. Just like exercising your physical muscles, you need to do it correctly. If an exercise is not done correctly it can actually damage your muscle. When people work with others, they can either grow to a state of consistence growth and understanding or they can stop growing and become bitter towards others. Start becoming more observant of yourself when you deal with people. Feel the way you make others feel, and listen to what you say to others.

Practice haggling and bartering. This will help empower your communication by strengthening the value of what you have, and weakening the value of what another has which you want. You can go to flea markets, fairs, and various street vendors who haggle daily. This power can't guarantee you will get something at a lesser cost, but it is a great practice to try.

Similar to haggling, ask for discounts when you are buying something which you normally don't barter for. Be creative, witty, and actually try to get the discount even if the say no. Try to convince the person who you are dealing with to give you a discount. Be persistent and have fun with it.

Go work a sales job for some time to strengthen your communication techniques. Salespeople need to work with the superhero power of communication every single day and taking on a sales job is a great way to quickly strengthen this ability. These jobs will be like learning to ride a bicycle, by putting the bicycle manual down and actually riding the bicycle. Once you learn a skill you can keep it with you.

You can observe, analyze and learn from others who are powerful communicators. For example, spend time around motivational speakers, lawyers, salespeople, comedians, and politicians. Research people who persuade and make a powerful impact on others through nothing more than their use of words.

Mingle and party with people. Learn how to have a great time, as well as to help others have a great time. Learn how to express yourself and even make others laugh.

Read up on various aspects of communication such as, body language, leadership, sales, how to express oneself emotionally around others, how to connect, relate, and bond with others. Those are just some of the many concepts which relate to communication.

Speak to another in their native language, a language which is not your own. By doing this you can learn the phonetics and flow of another genre of communication. It is also a great way to meet people, and make them feel proud and grateful for their native tongue. People are usually very helpful to others with their language, and willing to teach it.

Traits that signify empowered communication:

You are comfortable in crowds.

Public presentation performance doesn't bother you.

You are good at bartering.

You can talk your way out of confrontations.

You can make people laugh.

Others feel at ease around you.

When you're with others, it is easy to find commonality.

Technology

"*Any sufficiently advanced technology is indistinguishable from magic.*"

-Arthur Clarke

What is the superhero power of technology?

The power of technology can be defined as the ability to utilize technology to your advantage. Technology is an extension of us. It is an external mechanism created and used for the convenience and benefit of people. Think of how you use technology everyday, your smart phone is a good place to start. You have a desire to keep in contact with various friends, coworkers, and mentors and you can use you technology power to stay in contact with them. Technology works in a harmonious dance to aid in various aspects of your life. You can harness the superhero power of technology to better understand yourself and also to build, innovate, and create future technologies for others to use.

What are the benefits of empowering technology?

The benefits of empowered technology range from being able to use a stove to cook a delicious meal to being able to build a spaceship and explore the milky way and beyond. So the benefits of using the superhero power of technology can be discovered by looking at the way you currently use technology. For example, observe how you use technology everyday. You call your family and friends on the phone, connect to others across the world via the internet, drive a car or using public transportation to get groceries, and so on. All of these are routine habits, which have become a part of lives. We forget that there was a time when none of this existed, no phones, no cars, no running water, heated homes or air conditioning. Begin to understand how much technology assists you throughout the hours of your life. Find a place of gratitude in technology and you will be grateful all day long!

Self-discovery with technology:

Here are some questions regarding the power of technology. Questions I ask myself to better understand how to incorporate this power into my life, and how it can be used as an aid in bringing me closer to my goals, desires, and dreams. You can also have the chance to exercise your imagination, by envisioning possible futures of what we may have access through technology. It is a fun exercise to think about what kind of technology you wish to co-exist with in the future. The benefits and reasons to use technology are limitless, so the best thing to do is find out the benefits and reasons for technology in your life.

How has using technology enhanced my life?

What aspects of technology do I wish to understand and utilize?

What kind of technology would I like to have access to in the future?

How dependent on technology am I?

Fun ideas regarding technology:

Technology innovates and grows exponentially greater than most peoples' ability to understand it. Our power of technology is actually an extension of ourselves, it is something that develops so fast, it is nearly impossible for most to predict how they can utilize their power of technology in the future. For example, my Great Grandmother, being born in the early 20th century, witnessed the rapid growth of the transportation industry. She witnessed the birth and growth of cars and planes in a short amount of time. The same kind of technological growth can be said of telephones. Many people grew up without a mobile phone and just with payphones and home phones. The phone industry also experienced groundbreaking innovation. The idea of a mobile phone used to be mindboggling for most people, but think about how common they are today.

I wonder how I will be able to utilize my superhero power of technology in the future. Maybe I will be able to use it to understand a teleportation machine, like a car, but instead use it to travel wherever, whenever I want in a split second. It can be fun and also terrifying to think about the future of technology.

Your power of technology may need the assistance of other powers to strengthen it. For example, an old grandmother who has little experience with computers wants to know how to send an email. She can use her superhero power of action to find someone to teach her, or better yet, she can try to figure out how to do it on her own.

Daily practices to empower technology:

Most of us use technology every day when we use our electronics. If you want to strengthen your superhero power of technology, ask yourself how you would like to improve your life. Contemplate what you would like to learn and improve upon and research ways technology can help.

We use technology daily for various purposes, and in our use, we strengthen the superhero power of technology. Consider whatever technology you want to become more familiar with and simply make a commitment to learn it. Use it, play with it, discover how it works and you will be able to create positive change in your life.

Become a student, make the decision to learn more about technology. Take courses on technology, learn online or in person. Learn from a mentor, a friend, a relative, a teacher, or whoever is qualified with a sufficient amount of knowledge about what you're learning. Make it a practice to learn one new aspect of technology a month, or even once a day.

Traits that signify an empowered ability to learn and embrace technology:

You can utilize technology easily and efficiently.

You can create and/or innovate technology.

You are capable of using technology independently.

You can utilize technology as a means of expression. To express ideas, thoughts, and visions.

You keep in contact with people you haven't seen in a while.

Action

"*The path to success is to take massive, determined action.*"

-Anthony Robbins

What is the superhero power of action?

Action can be defined as the process of thinking about doing something, and then doing it. Taking action is a superhero power similar to a spark. A spark stands between a fireless chimney and a hot fiery blazed chimney. Action stand between imagining you dreams and actually living them.

What are the benefits of empowered action?

One benefit to having empowered action is you get things accomplished. Some people struggle with this superhero power and instead give it away to the control of others. For example, a student named Will wants to be a great pianist and conductor. Will gets exceptional grades and excels in mathematics. His parents, teacher, and guidance counselors encourage him to go to college to become an accountant, but all he wants to do is play music. I don't feel bad about Will pursuing an accountant job, but I would be inspired by him if he relentlessly pursued his passion and wielded the superhero power of action to manifest his dreams. Even better, maybe he could take super action and do both. It is important to listen to the life advice of others, to a certain extent, but we cannot allow others to make decisions for us. We can benefit greatly if we listen to our intuition and hearts and take action. Sometimes we have jobs that help us survive or are a means to an end. However, do not define job dissatisfaction as your life or even your ideal career path. A career can be a lifestyle, a way to make a living, but whatever path you chose, it's going to require a commitment and positive attitude. The main benefit to empowering your action is that you can recognize it as currency and see how you distribute it amongst you own beliefs and others' beliefs. More importantly, use the superhero power of action to propel yourself towards your goals, desires, passions, and dreams.

Self-discovery with action:

Here are a few questions to ask yourself, so that you can better understand your current relationship with action. Action is like currency and self-awareness about action is akin to viewing your checking account balance. For example, you access your checking account statement to see how much money you have and to ponder how you wish to spend it. In this same way, self-awareness can help you understand where you are spending your action energy. Are those activities empowering you or distracting you from your success? Ask yourself the following questions to see how much time you have to take action on things and then spend your action power accordingly. Balance your activity and energy budgets, by making time for the things which make you happy and make you feel like you're doing what is right for you.

Do I have control of my actions?

Do I allow others to tell me what actions to take?

Am I taking action on my highest excitement?

What prevents me from taking action?

Are my actions in align with my goals, passions, and dreams?

Fun ideas regarding action:

Action is a kind of magic. We have and use it as a force to accomplish, manifest and switch on our power to create. Our power of action is relative to our will. You can will things into existence. Taking action is a dance of will you perform to conjure those desires you have in your mind into your manifestation.

Daily practices to empower action:

A great and easy way to practice empowered action daily is by monitoring your food and beverage choices. While you do this, try to make a decision based on what you really want. This can be used in any situation, with what you want to do, with what you eat, and with what you want to think about. The point is to take action on your highest desire within reason. Don't overeat or eat things that you will regret, but take some time to figure out what would really nourish you at that moment in time.

To elaborate on the first practice, you can decide upon how you would like to spend your free time. Think and feel all your options and commit to what you are most excited about doing. It can be a reoccurring thing or something totally new. Some individuals tend to take action out of obligation and habit. Doing things out of habit and obligation is not always the best choice. For example, I have attended family as well as cultural gatherings which I did not want to go to was dissatisfied with the majority of my time spent there, but I did it out of obligation. Some events are great to attend, even if you aren't excited to go, because it keeps a strong bond between you and your loved ones. Not all of the family or cultural events that fill up our free time are crucially important. Sometimes it is better to say "no thank you" and take of yourself, be selective, it's okay to say "no" sometimes.

Think about some aspect about you that you would like to improve upon. For some it may be eating healthy, exercising, or even just being nicer to others. Find what it is you need to do to make those nagging life improvements. Once you know what you have to do, be strong and take action! One great example is exercising! Many people want to exercise but do not. A great daily practice for someone wishing to workout is to eliminate their procrastination and actually go workout. Make a commitment to exercise four times a week. Don't spend anytime negotiating with your laziness, if you want something don't hesitate, take action.

Traits that signify an empowered ability to take action:

You don't make excuses.

You accomplish tasks on time or ahead of schedule.

You understand the difference between desires and wants.

You accomplish your goals.

You inspire, and motivate others.

You are a leader.

Persistence

"Nothing in the world can take the place of persistence. Talent will not; nothing is more common than unsuccessful men with talent. Genius will not... Education will not... Persistence and determination alone are omnipotent..."

-Calvin Coolidge

What is the superhero power of persistence?

Persistence gives us strength to not give up. Persistence is a power people possesses that allows them to continue striving towards something even though it may be challenging. Persistence is when we pedal a bicycle to get somewhere. You must be persistent when peddling to keep the bike moving, otherwise you won't get to where you want to go. Persistence can be a challenging power to harness and grow. It certainly is one of the most important powers when someone is striving to accomplish a goal.

When it comes to achieving goals, persistence is that energy between the decision to chase a goal, and that goal being accomplished.

A great word which can be used to understand persistence is resilience; they seem to be two sides of the same coin. Think about a boxer with the goal of winning the boxing match. His jabs, hooks, uppercuts, and his ability to keep pushing it round after round is persistence. His ability to withstand and overcome all the punches, knock downs, and tiredness is resilience.

What are the benefits of empowered persistence?

One benefit of persistence, which may be the most important, is that it allows people to accomplish their goals, even when they may seem to be near impossible. Most successful people in life have needed persistence in the past. It continues, though, to be a driving force even after they achieve their dream, as it helps them avoid failure and doubt when they reach their personal summit. Those with the superhero power of persistence overcome difficult obstacles, and always strive to believe in themselves. Those with the most success sometimes go through the most rejection and disappointments. However, it is their own power of persistence that lifts up their mind, body, and spirit each time life knocks them down. Other brilliant thing successful people do, is that they avoid defining themselves as a failure. No matter how many times they fail, they never perceive themselves as such. Instead they perceive the shortcoming as a necessary part of their success.

Self-discovery with persistence:

Ask yourself these questions to investigate where the superhero power of persistence is in your life. Your answers may even help spark the power of persistence fire within you.

How has persistence served me?

How has lack of persistence served me?

What can you achieve with persistence?

Who is persistent in your life?

What exists within my life that makes me continuously take action?

What goals do you have?

Fun ideas regarding persistence:

It is a fun thing, discovering what conjures our persistence. The reason it is so fun is because there is an infinite array of beliefs, reasons, and thoughts that drive people to be persistent. It can be passion, children, faith, family, money, or pleasure.

When striving for success, the power persistence plows through failures, and pushes us towards our success. Back to boxing...persistence plays a role in your life similar to the role a boxing coach plays for a professional boxer whose desire is to be a heavyweight champion. A boxing coach assists their boxer to consistently work hard. When the boxer fails, the coach uses this as a tool to educate the boxer on improvement areas. At times the boxer might feel upset with the coach because he's being pushed so much and worked so hard. Maybe the boxer approaches the brink of quitting, but the coach motivates the boxer to persist. You are like the boxer, and whatever success you are striving to achieve is like the boxer's goal of being a heavyweight champion. Your power of persistence is the boxing coach, consistently pushing you to be better and better while simultaneously motivating you to never give up. Any failures you experience on your road to success are your tools and they are there for you to learn from and improve upon. Here's a great quote by

Zig Ziglar who once said, "Remember failure is an event not a person." This quote exemplifies how to preserve and recall your personal aspirations through persistence.

Daily practices to empower persistence:

Create a goal sheet, or visualize your goals and do something everyday in the direction towards accomplishing them. If you have physical goals make it apparent that you go to the gym or go for a jog every day. If it is a creative project or intellectual goal, then dedicate a part of your day, towards completing it.

Another great practice is to challenge laziness. When you really want to accomplish something, but for whatever reason you don't feel like working to accomplish it, challenge your attitude by questioning yourself. Ask yourself what your goals are, and if being lazy will get you to accomplish your goal. Ask yourself if you will be happy one year, two years, and five years from now if you let your laziness control your actions and decisions in life.

Try consciously recognizing your laziness, name it and don't let it get control of you or consume you. Make the choice to be persistent with your goals, move forward, progress, and succeed. Recognize that if you are extremely sluggish towards your goals then maybe you don't want to achieve those goals anyways. Rethink what you want out of life, and recreate some goals that you are actually excited and passionate to accomplish.

When you feel you want to give up on something you love, think of your options, which are: to quit, or keep trying. However, note that you may fail at either option you chose, but the only thing we know for sure is that the quitting option is a guaranteed fail. So for you to take the leap of faith and keep trying as much as you can, you automatically better your chances of success with the mere intention of it. Remember you have nothing to lose by trying. If you love something, then go for it!

Use of power-filled affirmations can help maintain the power of persistence within you. The great author, and motivational speaker Les Brown says, "It's not over until I win!" I find this statement to be both effective and impactful, as it immediately empowers the persistence within me. Find or create an affirmation that ignites the fires of passion within you. And use that affirmation to maintain strong persistence.

Another way to strengthen your superhero power of persistence is by exercising. Push yourself to the breaking point, where you want to quit, then keep on pushing and see how much extra energy you have.

Try meditating and observe how your persistence muscle can strengthen when you take on this challenge of quieting your mind. When meditating, have a goa of maybe 10 minutes. Do not let your mind take over the practice or convince you to give up. Test your meditation persistence with this exercise. Imagine a blank wall, black board, or empty table, think about that empty platform and leave it blank for as long as possible.

Make a goal for yourself within reason and work towards it until you accomplish it. A way to tackle larger and more challenging goals is to make mini goals that can be attained easily and that work towards the larger goal. Once one successfully accomplishes a larger personal goal, they will certainly have a stronger muscle of persistence and will be able to overcome challenges more easily.

Traits that signify empowered persistence:

You are self-motivated.

You are confident.

You are hard-working.

You tend to inspire others.

You do not give up easily on your goals, desires, and dreams, but surrender when you need to change course

Conclusion

Each of the superhero powers for daily life can be utilized in several ways to help you accomplish your goals, and manifest the life of your dreams. The powers have been created to be used as your personal tools. They can help you better understand your inner world. It's kind of like being given a microscope and a telescope for your life, so you can understand the invisible realms of your life from a detailed perspective, to one that is on a macro level. Once you start to learn how to use your superhero powers in daily life, you will be able to gain perspective by zoom in and out fluidly and naturally. This will help you gain a deeper understanding of yourself, your friends and family and life in general. You have been given the gift of life to achieve greatness, and this, ultimately is one of the greatest powers you have.

Your life is similar to a musical symphony. The superhero powers you can wield are similar to instruments being played; sometimes alone, sometimes all together, as well as in various different combinations. All of your instruments are there to be used and expressed throughout the stream of moments in your musical symphony. You can let the flutes (communication) be played during your job interview, or let the harp (patience) to be plucked while watching your kids or doing chores. The instruments are all ready to be expressed at any moment in time. You play as the composer of your musical symphony, fusing all the instrument sounds together to build a unified orchestra. So imagine yourself as brilliant composer who wants to create the most beautiful music ensemble that's ever been created. You use different combinations of instruments throughout your performance and actually produce the greatest music ensemble ever created. Then, once formed, you decide to record it, share it, and allow others to experience it. Imagine using different combinations of your newly learned superpowers for daily life throughout your time on earth to accomplish your goals. Now imagine living the life of your dreams, what would you be doing? Who would you be with? Where would you be?

Use your inner 14 real life superpowers to ignite the metaphoric process of your transformation into the greatest human being you can be. Use the powers to continuously grow and evolve into greater and more magnificent versions of yourself as time goes on. Others will look up to you as a powerful individual who manifested the life of their dreams, no matter what challenges or obstacles stood in their way. You will become an inspiration, and a source of motivation for others. You will become the greatest you. A real life superhero!

Why I Wrote this Book

I decided to organize these concepts and ideas and write them down because I needed help. I needed help with a few different aspects of my life. I needed help to the point where I could feel the weight of time and circumstance pinning me to the ground. I felt powerless and feeling powerless doesn't enhance anyone's life. Being powerless has no value. The feeling of being powerless is a sad burden to bestow upon yourself. If you have ever felt powerless, you may have noticed yourself caught in a repetitive cycle. I was in such a cycle, making myself the victim of several negative unforeseen situations and circumstances. I refer to it as a cycle because when the situations and circumstances occur they bring about suffering in order to justify the powerless feeling. Then the feeling is maintained until another unforeseen negative situation or circumstance occurs, thus justifying the powerless feeling again. It is a difficult trap to fall into, but many people who feel powerless actually have access to a reservoir of internal strength that can change their lives for the better.

For example, I have a strong desire to be an empowered individual and to collaborate with others whom share common goals of achieving success, but this wasn't always how I felt about my life. Today, I know I will wake up and tap into a vast range of pathways to achieve success, such as personal education, emotional well-being, career development, and a commitment to my health and financial goals. Self-empowerment is a simple decision when you think about it, but you have to make the choice. When you do decide to empower yourself, you may feel a burst of energy. This feeling is similar to when someone creates a goal and is committed to reaching it; the journey towards a goal can act like a magnet and create its own momentum. This motion can bring someone closer to their goal. When I first experienced this burst of energy, I felt immediate inspiration, passion, gratitude, and joy. The experience felt as if there was an invisible fountain that was spewing out energy, energy that I soaked up with the gratitude of a man, stranded in the desert, who has finally found some water. When you become an empowered individual, you can access this energy fountain whenever and wherever you happen to be.

This invisible energy fountain can be enhanced by a combination of the following:

1. A decision to become empowered
2. Dedication to the discovering, learning, and exploring of a passion
3. Creation of a list of goals
4. A persistent action towards those passions and/or goals

The energy gained from this formula can lift you up to a point where you can feel a gravitational pull bringing you closer to your goals and passions. When this force strengthens, your need to push yourself becomes less and less.

I enjoy reading and watching various self-help and motivational seminars, but what I really needed in my time of feeling powerless was a concept which I could relate to and for that concept to be interactive and fun. This book has been a way for me to organize all the value I have found through what I learned from others and through what I have learned from direct experience. I wrote this book as a way to liberate and empower myself. I tend to find analogies the easiest way to explain things; overall, this book is an analogy that enables people to channel their inner superheroes.

Growing up, I always had a strong fascination and obsession with superheroes. I love how they each share a similar quality, which is that they have discovered a great power within themselves. The fact that they make a choice to better serve humanity with this newfound power is the kicker, pun intended. Through the program relayed in this book, I was able to discover my inner super powers and to learn how I could better serve myself and others.

Through my self-help research, studies, and experience, I learned about my true and real powers, powers which we all possess. I so wanted to be my own superhero in my life. I wanted to be an inspiring, protective, and loving father to my two sons. I wanted to be a creator and contributor to life. I wanted to explore and learn about all of my interests and passions. I wanted to help people in as many ways as I am capable. And I wanted to help others who are ready to feel the same...and I figured out how to do this!

I want to share this with you and for you to feel powerful right now. I want you to be the person you want to be. I want to live amongst a world full of super-hero-people who contribute to themselves, others, and the world. I believe we all have the capability to be a superhero we just have to know where and how to locate our powers, how to strengthen our powers, and how to best use them.

All of our inherent strengths are transparent and will always be there for us. All of your powers can be used in harmony with one another, some powers even assist other powers in the process. Similar to the phenomena of light, each power is like a colored light wave. When all the light beams of color are radiating, aligned together, they make white light. All of our powers combined make a kind of light essence, a pure unified state of empowerment. Your powers are like a collection of human attributes which can either work for you or not. Once you understand your powers and how to exercise those abilities, you can better achieve your goals and desires.

Within every single person lies certain abilities, some that we are aware of and some that we have yet to discover. These capabilities attribute to the creative process of our existence. I hope this book will help you become conscious of your hidden powers and potential. I hope you gain a newly heightened perspective on your own mind and yourself, as well as most other aspects of life. When you put the effort in to strengthen each power, results are inevitable. You can and should use this book as a tool to help your drive yourself towards the manifestation of your desires, goals, and dreams. This is your life and your experience to create. How would it make you feel to be the superhero of your world? If you could do anything with this life what would you do? How will you like to be remembered? How can you contribute to humanity? What are your strengths? What is your passion? What is your fire? All these questions are great examples of what you can be asking yourself to help clarify what you would like out of life.

A collective goal for the human race that should be embraced and relentlessly pursued is to work together towards making the world a more secure, loving, intelligent, fun, compatible place. After reading this book, I wish for you that your inner powers inspire you to take action to achieve your greatest dream. I hope this book will help you learn how to overcome challenges everyone faces on the road to success. Lastly, I have created a system that teaches people to overcome obstacles which work against their powers and it has worked for many, many individuals so far.

Imagine the world is a big party and our job is to make the party is safe, fun, loving, accepting, and empowering. How do you feel when you can contribute to this party? And how would you like to experience the party?

Answering these questions will help you attain your desires, goals, and dreams. The idea is to utilize as many of your personal powers simultaneously. In doing so, I know you will become an inspiration towards yourself and others.

So go out into the world and be your own superhero.

Made in the USA
Charleston, SC
23 February 2016